VIRGINIA TECH
HOKIES

BY JEFF SEIDEL

SportsZone

An Imprint of Abdo Publishing
abdopublishing.com

abdopublishing.com

Published by Abdo Publishing, a division of ABDO, PO Box 398166, Minneapolis, Minnesota 55439.
Copyright © 2019 by Abdo Consulting Group, Inc. International copyrights reserved in all countries.
No part of this book may be reproduced in any form without written permission from the publisher.
SportsZone™ is a trademark and logo of Abdo Publishing.

Printed in the United States of America, North Mankato, Minnesota
032018
092018

Cover Photo: Bob Leverone/AP Images
Interior Photos: Bob Leverone/AP Images, 1; Al Messerschmidt/AP Images, 4–5; Simon Bruty/Sports
Illustrated/Getty Images, 6; Doug Pensinger/Allsport/Getty Images Sport, 8; Damian Strohmeyer/
Sports Illustrated/Getty Images, 11; AP Images, 12; S. Shepard/iStockphoto, 14–15; Fred Kfoury III/Icon
Sportswire482/Newscom, 17; Robert Riger/Hulton Archive/Getty Images, 19; Steve Helber/AP Images,
20–21, 32–33, 36–37, 41, 43 (top), 43 (bottom left), 43 (bottom right), 44; Virginia Tech/Collegiate
Images/Getty Images, 22, 43 (bottom middle); Steve Helber/AP Images, 24; Peter Reed Miller/Sports
Illustrated/Getty Images, 26–27, 42 (left); Brian Snyder/Reuters/Newscom, 29; Mike Segar/Reuters/
Newscom, 31, 42 (right); Chris O'Meara/AP Images, 35; Lee Coleman/Icon Sportswire/AP Images, 38

Editor: Patrick Donnelly
Series Designer: Craig Hinton

Library of Congress Control Number: 2017962141

Publisher's Cataloging-in-Publication Data

Names: Seidel, Jeff, author.
Title: Virginia Tech Hokies / by Jeff Seidel.
Description: Minneapolis, Minnesota : Abdo Publishing, 2019. | Series: Inside college football | Includes
    online resources and index.
Identifiers: ISBN 9781532114632 (lib.bdg.) | ISBN 9781532154461 (ebook)
Subjects: LCSH: American football--Juvenile literature. | College sports--United States--
    History--Juvenile literature. | Virginia Tech Hokies (Football team)--Juvenile literature. |
    Football--Records--United States--Juvenile literature.
Classification: DDC 796.332630--dc23

TABLE OF CONTENTS

Michael Vick burst onto the scene with the Hokies in 1999.

A SEASON TO REMEMBER

MICHAEL VICK BECAME THE STORY OF THE VIRGINIA TECH SEASON IN 1999. HIS DYNAMIC RUNNING AND PASSING SKILLS MADE HIM THE FOCUS OF HIGHLIGHT SHOWS FROM COAST TO COAST. BUT HE WAS STILL A MYSTERY TO MOST HOKIES FANS WHEN THE SEASON BEGAN.

Virginia Tech was ranked No. 13 in the country when Vick made his collegiate debut in the season opener, a 47–0 victory over James Madison. The 19-year-old had already spent one year on campus in Blacksburg, Virginia. He was a redshirt. That meant he could practice but not play in games. The next fall, Vick was eager to show what he had learned.

It didn't take long for Vick to get people talking. He rushed for three touchdowns against James Madison—in the first half. On the last one, he did an eye-popping flip into the end zone. He sprained an ankle and had to sit out the rest of the game. But Hokies fans were excited about his potential.

Vick rolls out to his left, looking for an
open receiver.

The injury kept Vick on the sidelines the next week as the Hokies

beat Alabama-Birmingham. He returned in time to help his teammates

beat Clemson on a nationally televised Thursday night game. In the next

three weeks, Vick and the Hokies knocked off Virginia, Rutgers, and

Syracuse. The offense posted an eye-popping 120 points over the latter

two games. Virginia Tech now stood at No. 3 in the national poll and was

starting to dream big.

"I'm sold," Virginia Tech receiver Ricky Hall said after the Hokies drubbed 16th-ranked Syracuse 62–0. "I'm pretty sure we can go out there and play with anybody."

They remained at No. 3 after beating Pittsburgh 30–17. That set up a battle with archrival West Virginia. The Hokies were 7–0 when they traveled to Morgantown, West Virginia. But late in the game, their perfect record was in jeopardy.

Tech trailed 20–19 when it took over on its own 15-yard line with just over a minute to play. Vick took control. The freshman quarterback completed two quick passes, moving the ball to the Hokies' 38-yard line with 35 seconds left.

Then Vick made the play that saved Virginia Tech's season. With precious seconds slipping away, Vick avoided a heavy pass rush and rolled out to his right. But he couldn't find an open receiver. He appeared to be running out of bounds at the Virginia Tech 40.

But Vick fooled everyone, especially the West Virginia defenders. Instead of going out of bounds, he darted down the sideline. With the speed of an Olympic sprinter, Vick raced 25 yards in the blink of an eye. He was finally forced out of bounds at the West Virginia 36.

One more completion for 9 yards put the ball on the West Virginia 27-yard line. Senior kicker Shayne Graham trotted onto the field to attempt a game-winning 44-yard field goal. The Virginia Tech sideline was tense. Some teammates laid on their stomachs—perhaps in prayer, perhaps because they couldn't bear to watch.

They had no reason to worry. Graham calmly booted the ball through the uprights. Virginia Tech won 22–20. The game would come to be known as the "Miracle in Morgantown." The Hokies became the first 8–0 football team at the school in 94 years. They also remained on track in their quest for the school's first national championship.

The last three regular-season games were easy wins. They routed No. 19 Miami, Temple, and 22nd-ranked Boston College. Virginia Tech finished the regular season ranked No. 2 in the land, unbeaten and untied for the first time since 1918.

The 11–0 regular season earned the Hokies a chance to play in the Sugar Bowl. Vick and Virginia Tech would meet top-ranked Florida State with the national championship on the line. Vick had led the Hokies' talented roster all season long. The question remained whether they could pull off one more victory.

The Hokies ran into early trouble on special teams. Florida State blocked a punt that was returned for a touchdown. Then Seminoles star receiver Peter Warrick returned a punt 59 yards for another touchdown. Florida State led 28–7 late in the second quarter. It looked like the Hokies' dream season would end in an embarrassing blowout loss.

DON'T FORGET ABOUT COREY

Senior defensive end Corey Moore also had a spectacular 1999 season for Virginia Tech. He won the Bronko Nagurski Trophy as the best defensive player in the nation. Moore also captured the Lombardi Award as the college football lineman of the year. He also was a unanimous first-team All-American, the first Hokie defensive player to earn that honor.

The numbers certainly show what a great season he turned in. Moore finished with 60 tackles, 17 sacks, and 11 tackles for a loss. He added 25 hurries—when the quarterback has to get rid of the ball because he's under pressure. Moore also forced three fumbles and returned a fumble for a touchdown. And he did all of that despite standing just a hair under 6 feet (183 cm).

"You don't see many 6-footers around that can change the game the way Corey can," coach Frank Beamer said. "In his anticipation of the snap he gains a half-step, and then there's no one fast enough to catch him. If you use one guy on him, you can't block him."

Then Vick went to work, doing his thing just as he'd done against West Virginia and everyone else. He darted in all directions and made numerous Seminoles miss tackles on a 43-yard dash. That set up his 3-yard touchdown run that cut the lead to 28–14 at halftime.

BY THE NUMBERS

There was a bit of an age difference between the two quarterbacks in that Sugar Bowl game. Michael Vick was 19 years old, a redshirt freshman for Virginia Tech. Chris Weinke of Florida State had played minor league baseball for six years after high school. He didn't begin college until much later in life. Weinke was 27 years old when he faced the Hokies.

The Hokies came out and dominated the third quarter. Graham kicked a field goal. Then running back Andre Kendrick scored two touchdowns. The comeback was complete. Virginia Tech led 29–28 heading into the final period. The national championship was in sight.

However, the Seminoles were a veteran team. They weren't rattled by Virginia Tech's 22-point comeback. Florida State scored the game's final 18 points to ward off the upset-minded Hokies. Warrick's third touchdown of the game, a 43-yard pass from Heisman Trophy–winning quarterback Chris Weinke, sealed the win. The Seminoles claimed a 46–29 victory and their second national title.

Still, it was an impressive showing by Vick and the Hokies. They put up 503 yards of total offense. Vick turned in an amazing individual effort in the loss. He ran for 97 yards on 23 carries and completed 15 of 29 passes for 225 yards and a touchdown. That's 322 yards of total offense.

Like many Virginia Tech opponents that season, the Seminoles had no answer for the talented quarterback.

Vick established himself as a true double threat that season. He dazzled defenders with his shifty running, amassing 682 yards and nine touchdowns on the ground. He also passed over them with his strong and accurate left arm. Vick completed 105 of 182 passes for 2,065 yards and 13 touchdowns with just five interceptions. And he led the country in yards per passing attempt, meaning he made the most of his

[11]

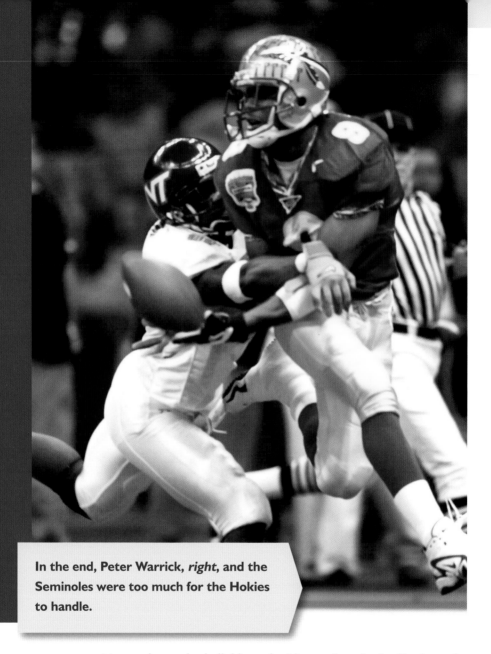

In the end, Peter Warrick, *right*, and the Seminoles were too much for the Hokies to handle.

opportunities to throw the ball. He and wide receiver Andre Davis made for an explosive duo that season. Davis caught 42 passes for 1,070 yards and 10 touchdowns. His per-catch average of 25.5 yards led the nation.

Vick said in an interview during the 1999 season that sitting out a year had taught him a few lessons and made him a better player.

"At first I didn't take things seriously last year, so it was good that I was sitting," Vick said. "[Now] I'm serious about every part of the job. People are saying I was the missing piece."

Virginia Tech adopted a slogan that nearly came true during the 1999 season. A sign saying "Preparing to Win a National Championship" was taped to a door in the football offices, written in simple block letters. The Hokies came 15 minutes away from making that happen. They finished the season ranked No. 2 in the nation. And they put the rest of the country on notice that the team in Blacksburg takes its football seriously.

TROPHY GAMES

The Hokies' main traditional rivals are West Virginia and Virginia, and a unique trophy is on the line whenever they square off. Because both schools are located in the heart of coal country, Virginia Tech and West Virginia play for the Black Diamond Trophy. Meanwhile, the Hokies and Virginia Cavaliers battle for the Commonwealth Cup, which represents bragging rights as the best college football team in Virginia.

Lane Stadium has been the Hokies' home field since 1965.

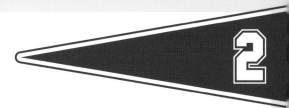

2

THE EARLY DAYS

THE GROWTH OF VIRGINIA TECH FOOTBALL WAS A SLOW PROCESS. IT BEGAN IN 1891, WHEN THE SCHOOL WAS CALLED THE VIRGINIA AGRICULTURAL AND MECHANICAL (A&M) COLLEGE. SCHOOL PRESIDENT JOHN MCBRYDE AGREED TO BEGIN AN ATHLETIC ASSOCIATION ON CAMPUS.

A group of students and faculty members came together to play informal games of football that fall. The next year brought more interest, and the team began playing other schools. The first official football game took place on campus on October 21, 1892. Virginia A&M scored a 14–10 victory over St. Albans of Radford, Virginia. Professor W. E. Anderson scored the game-winning touchdown.

Professor E. A. Smyth studied the rules for the new sport and became its trainer. He was basically the team's coach and business manager. He came to be known as the father of football at Virginia Tech.

The Bugle, the school yearbook, reported on the first football practices in 1892: "[W]e had some fun . . . suits were ordered, footballs of various descriptions bought and general enthusiasm prevailed."

Hunter Carpenter became one of the best-known players in the school's early years. He played at Virginia Tech between 1900 and 1905. He was only 15 and weighed 128 pounds when he arrived on campus. Carpenter did not play much during his first two seasons. But he helped Virginia Tech beat Navy 11–0 in 1903 by kicking a 46-yard field goal.

Carpenter led Virginia Tech to a 9–1 record in 1905 as the Hokies outscored their opponents 305–24. In 1957 he was inducted into the College Football Hall of Fame.

The Hokies won more games than they lost every year between 1902 and 1914. They even went 7–0 in 1918, allowing just 13 points all season. But they did not find much other success in those early years. In 1954 they finished with an 8–0–1 record but were edged out for the Southern Conference championship by rival West Virginia. The Hokies finally ended their drought in 1963, when they won their first and only Southern Conference title.

One of the biggest wins that season came when the Hokies

GOBBLE, GOBBLE

A Hokie is a mythical bird that looks kind of like a turkey. Virginia Tech fans have called their team the "Fighting Gobblers" for years. And the first Virginia Tech mascot truly was a gobbler—a real turkey that local character Floyd "Hard Times" Meade brought to the sidelines during the 1912 season.

defeated Florida State on the road 31–23. Newt Green blocked a punt; Jake Adams picked the ball out of the air and ran it 38 yards for a crucial touchdown. Another big win was a 14–13 decision at Richmond. Mike Cahill intercepted a two-point conversion pass to help lock up that win.

Construction on Lane Stadium began in April 1964, and the team's new home was finally completed four years later. But the Hokies started playing games there before the project was finished. Virginia Tech beat the College of William & Mary 9–7 on October 2, 1965, in the first game at Lane Stadium. At that point, just a few parts of the stadium had been completed—seats had been installed only in the west stands and the center section of the east bleachers. Eventually the rest of the stands were filled in, and numerous additions and changes have been made in the years since.

Virginia Tech earned berths in the Liberty Bowl in 1966 and 1968. Future coach Frank Beamer played on both of these teams as a defensive back. Miami beat the Hokies 14–7 in the 1966 game. Mississippi topped Virginia Tech 34–17 in the other.

Jerry Claiborne was the coach at that time. A few years later, he left to become the head coach at Maryland, and he later resurrected the failing program at Kentucky as well.

HOKIES TOGETHER

Offensive linemen Buzz Nutter and George Preas both played for the Hokies in the 1950s. They later went on to help the Baltimore Colts to two National Football League (NFL) titles. Nutter was the center in the famous 1958 NFL Championship Game in which the Colts beat the New York Giants 23–17 in overtime. Nutter made numerous key blocks and plays in the late minutes of the game. He took pride in working hard.

"I never missed a day of practice my whole football career—and sometimes it took a lot to get there," Nutter said in 2004. "If I could make it to practice, then I can make it to work."

Preas played right tackle and threw the key block on Alan Ameche's game-winning touchdown run. Both linemen were back the following year when the Colts repeated as NFL champions.

Bill Dooley turned things around at Virginia Tech when he took over as head coach in 1978. The Hokies had played in only five bowl games and lost all of them before Dooley led them to the Peach Bowl in 1986. Virginia Tech edged North Carolina State 25–24 that day for the school's first bowl victory.

Dooley was the head coach for nine seasons, and the Hokies had a winning record in the final seven. When he left in 1987 to take over the program at Wake Forest, Virginia Tech turned to Beamer. The former Hokie was coaching at Murray State University. That move turned out to be a pretty good one for Virginia Tech.

THE EARLY DAYS

Frank Beamer led the Hokies to new heights during his 29 years as head coach.

3

BEAMER BALL

FRANK BEAMER CAME FROM A TOWN NAMED FANCY GAP, VIRGINIA (POPULATION 237 IN 2010). IT'S LOCATED ROUGHLY 65 MILES (105 KM) SOUTH OF BLACKSBURG. THOUGH BEAMER LEFT FANCY GAP IN THE 1960s, THE LOCALS REMAIN PROUD OF THEIR FAVORITE SON. A SIGN ON US HIGHWAY 52 IN THE TOWN SAYS "WELCOME TO FANCY GAP, VA." AT THE TOP AND "FRANK BEAMER COUNTRY" AT THE BOTTOM.

Beamer played football at Hillsville High School in Fancy Gap before heading to Virginia Tech. He became a starting cornerback for the Hokies and helped lead them to the Liberty Bowl in 1966 and 1968. He then began working his way up the coaching ladder. Beamer was a high school assistant for three years and a college assistant at Maryland, The Citadel, and finally Murray State.

Murray State hired Beamer to be its defensive coordinator in 1979. He took over as head coach there in 1981. Over the next six years, Murray State went 42–23–2.

Bruce Smith was one of the fiercest pass rushers in the history of college and professional football.

In 1987 Beamer returned to Virginia Tech to replace head coach Bill Dooley, who had left him with a number of headaches to deal with. Dooley's staff was accused of multiple recruiting violations, and those allegations cast a shadow over Beamer's early years. The Hokies did not make a bowl game in his first six years as coach, and they had a record of just 24–40–2 during that time.

Virginia Tech fans were starting to grumble, especially after the team finished with a 2–8–1 record in 1992. They wanted to see their team going to bowl games, and the Hokies hadn't done that since Beamer took the job.

But the tide began to turn in 1993. Virginia Tech went 9–3 that season and beat Indiana in the Independence Bowl. The Hokies went 8–4 in 1994, losing to Tennessee in the Gator Bowl, but they were on their way. After not being invited to a bowl game in Beamer's first six years, they never missed again. The Hokies also won or shared three Big East titles before moving to the Atlantic Coast Conference (ACC) in 2004 and winning there, too.

BRUCE SMITH

Defensive end Bruce Smith left his mark on the Virginia Tech program during his four years in Blacksburg. A native of Norfolk, Virginia, Smith posted 46 quarterback sacks as a Hokie from 1981 to 1984. He burst into the national spotlight during his junior year. That year he earned first-team All-America honors with an amazing 22 sacks in 11 games. The next year he won the Outland Trophy as the best lineman in the country. He also helped lead the Hokies to the Independence Bowl.

The Buffalo Bills made Smith the first pick of the 1985 NFL Draft, and he didn't disappoint as a pro. He posted 15 sacks in his second season. That started a 13-year run in which he reached double figures in sacks in 12 seasons. He also was voted to the Pro Bowl 11 times and helped lead the Bills to four Super Bowls. Smith was inducted into the College Football Hall of Fame in 2006 and the Pro Football Hall of Fame in 2009.

Their best seasons were when quarterback Michael Vick ran the show in 1999 and 2000. Virginia Tech went 11–1 in each of those two seasons and reached the 1999 national championship game before falling to Florida State.

One aspect that helped Virginia Tech earn its reputation of success and exciting play was referred to as "Beamer Ball." Beamer loved to focus on special teams. His Hokies were known for making big plays defending and returning kicks and punts.

"We had so many games over the years turn on a punt return or a blocked field goal," Beamer said. "Special teams are the quickest way to win a football game. The better you are on special teams—regardless of what else you have on offense and defense—the better your chances of winning."

The Hokies blocked 66 kicks during the 1990s, more than any other Division I program. In Beamer's 29 years at Virginia Tech, the Hokies' special teams blocked 138 kicks. Even more incredible, they scored 55 special-teams touchdowns in that span. Those totals include 20 touchdowns from punt returns, 20 from blocked punts, nine kickoff returns, four blocked field goal returns, one fumbled kick recovery, and one fumbled kick return.

Beamer gave every coach on the Virginia Tech staff a role in the kicking game, and the hard work paid off.

GOING BOWLING

After not making many bowl games for nearly the first 100 years of their existence, the Hokies started becoming postseason regulars. They made a bowl game in 25 straight seasons from 1993 through 2017. At the time it was recognized as the longest active bowl streak in the country. Florida State had made 36 consecutive bowl appearances through 2017, but their 2006 Emerald Bowl appearance was forfeited due to academic violations.

BEAMER BALL

Vick frustrated Florida State's defense
with his shifty moves all night.

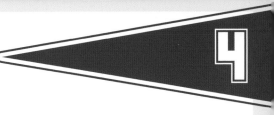

4

DUAL THREAT

ONE PLAY IN THE SUGAR BOWL AFTER THE 1999 SEASON SHOWED WHY QUARTERBACK MICHAEL VICK WAS SO DIFFICULT TO DEFEND. THE HOKIES WERE LOSING BY FIVE LATE IN THE THIRD QUARTER IN THE NATIONAL CHAMPIONSHIP GAME. THEY HAD THE BALL AT FLORIDA STATE'S 35-YARD LINE WHEN VICK TOOK THE SNAP AND WENT TO WORK.

He began by drifting to his left before quickly cutting back to the right and taking off. Several Florida State defenders chased him from all directions. But that didn't seem to bother Vick. He just kept moving.

Vick avoided more would-be tacklers before turning back toward the center of the field. Overall, the shifty Vick had made at least 10 Florida State defenders miss a tackle during the run. He somehow made his way to the Seminoles' 20-yard line, a play that seemed to leave television announcer Brent Musburger in shock as he described the play.

TROUBLED TIMES

Michael Vick had a long career in the NFL, first as a star with the Atlanta Falcons and later as a backup with the Philadelphia Eagles. But he tainted his legacy through bad decisions made away from football. His career was interrupted in 2007 when he was sent to federal prison for his involvement with a dogfighting operation. He was sentenced to 23 months. After his release, Vick worked to support laws that would make animal fighting illegal.

Vick learned in 2017 that he would be soon be inducted into the Virginia Tech Sports Hall of Fame. Some protests arose, but the ceremony went on as planned that September. "Everybody deserves a second chance, and what he did on the field has nothing to do with what he did off the field," one Virginia Tech student said. "That's why he's in the Hall of Fame."

"Vick, dashing back, here he comes again. Electrifying! First down at the 20-yard line. Fifteen more yards, and have you ever seen anything like this?" Musburger marveled.

Those plays were common for Vick, who proved to be a very uncommon quarterback during his two years at Virginia Tech. These days many college programs expect their quarterbacks to excel at both passing and running. However, that was not the trend when Vick played in college. In those days, a quarterback was known as either a passer or a runner. Few put both skills on display the way Vick did.

It didn't hurt that Vick had a strong arm and could throw the ball anywhere on the field with accuracy and timing. But he also could run like a sprinter. When timed at his pro day before the NFL Draft in 2001,

When Vick took off running he proved to be nearly impossible to contain.

Vick blazed through the 40-yard dash in 4.33 seconds. At Virginia Tech, he once was timed at 4.25 in the 40. Add to that straightaway speed an ability to quickly change directions, and you had a lethal package in the open field.

"Sometimes, we just hoped our receivers were covered so that Michael would have to scramble around and run," said coach Frank Beamer when looking back years later. "If the receivers were covered, that means they probably had quite a few people in coverage, so there's only so many people rushing the passer. If it's four or less, the odds are pretty good that Michael could pick up 10 yards if he broke out of there."

After leading Virginia Tech to the national title game as a redshirt freshman, Vick had another strong showing as a sophomore. The Hokies went 11–1 once again in 2000, and Vick threw for 1,234 yards with eight touchdown passes. He added 617 yards and eight touchdowns on the ground. The Hokies were ranked second in the country when Vick suffered a sprained ankle in a win over Pittsburgh. The next week, he missed most of a 20-point loss at No. 3 Miami, the only blemish on the Hokies' record.

Had Vick remained healthy, another shot at the national title might have been in the cards. Instead, Virginia Tech had to settle for whipping Clemson 41–20 in the Gator Bowl. The Hokies finished the season ranked No. 6 in the nation, thanks in large part to the incredible Vick.

"He just had a gift, an ability that he could run a little bit faster, jump a little bit quicker, had a great feel for the game," Beamer said. "How he threw the ball and how quickly it came out and how accurate he was. He could throw the touch pass over the middle, [and] he could throw the deep ball."

Those were big reasons why NFL teams wanted him. Vick entered the 2001 NFL Draft, and as sorry as the Hokies were to lose him, he was as sad to leave Virginia Tech.

NFL Commissioner Paul Tagliabue welcomes Vick to the NFL at the league's 2001 draft.

"This has been one of the hardest decisions I've ever had to make in my life," said Vick at the news conference when he announced his plans to leave college. The Atlanta Falcons selected him with the first pick in the NFL Draft, and the Hokies moved on to see what the post-Vick era would bring them.

DUAL THREAT

James Griffin holds a sign declaring the Hokies champions of the ACC after they beat Virginia to clinch the title in 2004.

MOVING TO THE COAST

SINCE THE 1960s THE ATLANTIC COAST CONFERENCE (ACC) HAS BEEN ONE OF THE TOP CONFERENCES FOR COLLEGE ATHLETICS. VIRGINIA TECH HAD LONG WANTED TO JOIN THE ACC, HOME TO IN-STATE RIVAL VIRGINIA. THERE WAS JUST ONE PROBLEM. THE ACC DID NOT WANT THE HOKIES.

Virginia Tech eventually got in, but the Hokies had to jump through a lot of hoops before receiving an invitation. The school applied to join the conference in the mid-1960s but did not get the support it needed from other schools. A few years later, Duke was thought to be leaving the conference. The Hokies thought they could get in then, but Duke didn't leave, and Virginia Tech remained independent.

South Carolina left for the Southeast Conference in 1971, but Georgia Tech was eventually chosen to fill that vacancy. After 26 years without a conference, Virginia Tech joined the Big East in 1991. But the Hokies didn't forget about the ACC.

INCREASING FOOTPRINT

The Hokies joined the ACC mostly for one reason: money. The ACC had said in 2003 that it wanted to expand the conference and find ways into larger TV markets. Blacksburg, Virginia, isn't a big city, so the ACC courted other Big East schools, such as Miami, Boston College, and Syracuse.

Then five schools in the Big East, including Virginia Tech, filed a lawsuit trying to stop the ACC from taking its schools. The Hokies, of course, dropped out of that when the ACC invited them into the conference.

Eventually the ACC added Miami, Boston College, Syracuse, and the Hokies. Pittsburgh and Louisville also joined later, while Notre Dame became a member of the ACC in all sports but football. The Fighting Irish give the conference a presence in the Chicago market. In addition, the conference footprint stretches along the Atlantic coast from Massachusetts to southern Florida.

In 2003 the ACC was looking to expand. The Hokies finally got an invitation to join the conference. "We know that this affiliation will be good for our students, athletes, fans and communities for years to come," Virginia Tech president Charles Steger said.

The Hokies officially joined the conference on July 1, 2004, and started play in the various sports that fall. Virginia Tech reportedly got support from Virginia governor Mark Warner, who pressured University of Virginia president John Casteen to support Virginia Tech's bid to join the ACC.

Though the ACC was believed to be a tougher conference than the Big East, the move worked out well for Virginia Tech in many ways, especially on the football field. The Hokies won the ACC championship in football four times in their first 13 seasons, and many players earned individual conference honors.

Beamer raises the ACC championship trophy after Virginia Tech won the 2008 conference title game.

Thanks to the move, the Hokies also did well off the field. College sports are becoming more and more about big money. Virginia Tech made more of that after shifting to the ACC. For example, the school said the football program had brought in $21.7 million in 2002. By 2006 that number nearly doubled to $40.75 million. That's an increase of 88 percent, something any business would enjoy.

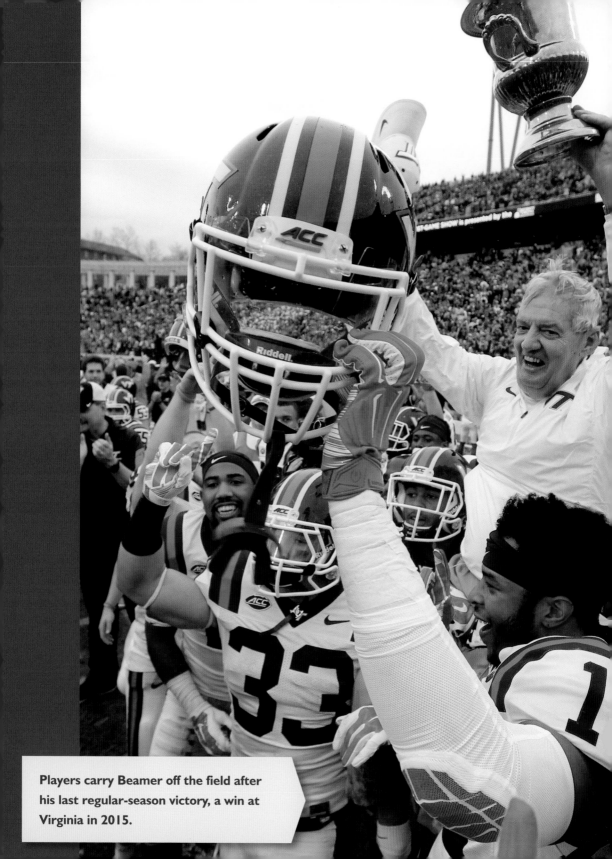

Players carry Beamer off the field after his last regular-season victory, a win at Virginia in 2015.

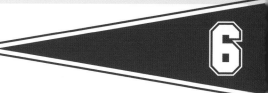

A NEW COACH

FRANK BEAMER TURNED VIRGINIA TECH INTO A NATIONAL POWERHOUSE DURING HIS 29 YEARS IN BLACKSBURG. THE HOKIES BECAME A TEAM WELL KNOWN TO ANYONE WHO FOLLOWED COLLEGE FOOTBALL.

Despite all of their success, the Hokies faded a bit during Beamer's last few years as head coach. They had won at least 10 games 11 times over a 13-year period from 1999 to 2011. After that, the results were not as good. Beamer had a 29–23 record during his last four seasons. When they began the 2015 season with a 4–5 record, Beamer said he would step down when the season ended.

"I've always said I think I'll know when it's time. And I think it's time," Beamer said at a press conference on November 2, 2015. "I think it's the right time."

The Hokies finished the season with a 7–6 record. And before Beamer left, the school found his replacement. As the

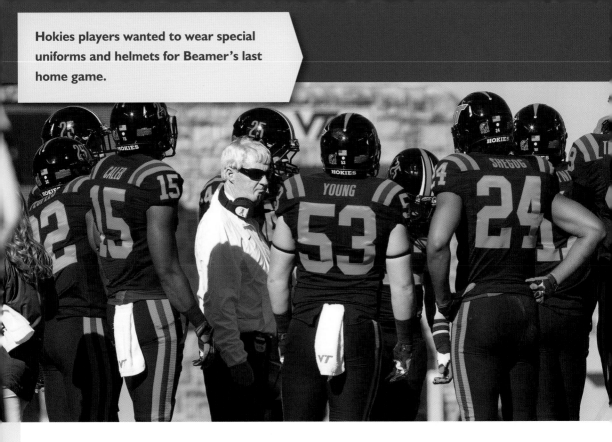

team prepared for the Independence Bowl, Virginia Tech announced that Memphis coach Justin Fuente would take over in Blacksburg.

Fuente played quarterback at Murray State for two years in the late 1990s after transferring from Oklahoma, where he had also spent two seasons. The move to Murray State proved to be a good one. Fuente rewrote the school's record book, setting single-season records with 3,498 passing yards, 400 pass attempts, 240 completions, and 27 touchdown passes. Those marks have since been broken, but Fuente still ranks in the top 10 in each category.

Beamer and Fuente met before Virginia Tech introduced Fuente as the new coach. Beamer used their Murray State connection to help break the ice. At a press conference the next day, the new coach joked that among his many coaching awards, Beamer picked out only one of them to show the new coach.

GOING OUT IN STYLE

As the Hokies prepared to play their last home game under Beamer, the players made an interesting request. They wanted to change their uniforms to an all-black scheme, including black helmets with the number 25 on them. That was Beamer's jersey number when he was a defensive back at Virginia Tech in the 1960s.

The players were fired up about it, though Beamer tried to play it down a little. "I just want them ready to play," Beamer said. "I don't care what they're playing in. If they like it, I like it. So let's just go play with them."

Unfortunately, despite the altered uniforms, Virginia Tech lost to North Carolina 30–27 in overtime. But in the Hokies' final game under Beamer, the 2015 Independence Bowl, they gave him a fitting sendoff. They beat Tulsa 55–52 in a wild shootout that, of course, included a 67-yard punt return for a touchdown by Virginia Tech's Greg Stroman.

It was a plaque he had received when being inducted into Murray State's Hall of Fame in 2004. That impressed Fuente, who noted that he hadn't received that honor yet. Fuente was honored by how welcoming Beamer had been in their visit and said he knew exactly what faced him in taking this job.

"We all know you don't replace a legend in coaching," Fuente said. "You hope to build on what he's already done. You hope to continue to operate in the same manner with the same principles and same integrity that he's done for so many years here."

Given Fuente's background as a quarterback, he hoped to jump-start a stagnant Hokies offense, and that's just what happened. They averaged 35 points per game in 2016. Because Virginia Tech already had a solid defense under longtime assistant coach Bud Foster, the move to Fuente proved to be a good one.

But the new coach knew he had the old coach in his corner. Fuente turned to Beamer late in the 2016 season when the Hokies needed to beat Virginia for a spot in the ACC championship game. He asked Beamer if he would talk with the Hokies the day before the game.

Beamer accepted the invitation and told the players that they had a big opportunity in front of them, to possibly play for the ACC title. He also said he was glad to see how smoothly things had gone for the team since the coaching change took place.

Virginia Tech crushed Virginia 52–10 but lost to Clemson in the ACC championship game. The Hokies then went on to beat Arkansas 35–24 in the Belk Bowl and finished with a 10–4 record in Fuente's first season.

The Hokies were ranked No. 16 in the final Associated Press poll, their best showing since 2010. The new coach had begun moving his team back to the highest levels of college football, a place it had been a number of times with its old coach.

TIMELINE

Virginia Tech begins its college football program, beating St. Albans of Radford, Virginia, in the school's first game.

The school's colors change from black and gray to maroon and burnt orange. The team wears them for the first time in a football game that fall.

The Hokies become a charter member of the Southern Intercollegiate Conference. Two years later, the name changes to simply the Southern Conference.

Hunter Carpenter, a Hokie from 1900 to 1903 and again in 1905, is inducted into the College Football Hall of Fame.

Virginia Tech leaves the Southern Conference to become an independent.

1892   1896   1921   1957   1965

Virginia Tech and Miami share the Big East title.

The Hokies share the Big East championship for a second straight season, this time with Miami and Syracuse.

Michael Vick concludes a spectacular redshirt freshman season by leading the Hokies to the national championship game. Florida State rallies late and hands Virginia Tech a 46–29 loss in the Sugar Bowl.

After leading the team to the Gator Bowl in his sophomore season, Vick decides to leave Virginia Tech to enter the NFL Draft, where Atlanta picks him first overall.

Virginia Tech officially gets invited to switch from the Big East to the Atlantic Coast Conference.

1995   1996   1999   2000   2003

Coach Jerry Claiborne's Hokies make it to the Liberty Bowl, where they lose to Miami 14–7.

The Hokies return to the Liberty Bowl, but Claiborne's team loses once more, this time to Mississippi. Archie Manning, Peyton's dad, plays quarterback for Ole Miss in the 34–17 win.

Frank Beamer is hired as head coach on December 22. Former coach Bill Dooley's final game is a 25–24 win over North Carolina in the Peach Bowl, the school's first bowl win.

After playing independently for 26 years, Virginia Tech joins the Big East Conference, which had just added football.

The Hokies beat Indiana 45–20 in the Independence Bowl.

1966 1968 1986 1991 1993

The Hokies win a football championship in their first year competing in the ACC.

Bruce Smith is inducted into the College Football Hall of Fame.

Virginia Tech wins its first of two straight ACC championships.

Beamer steps down at the end of the season following a 29-year run as head coach. Virginia Tech replaces him with Memphis coach Justin Fuente.

The Hokies go 10–4 in Fuente's first year as head coach as he improves the offense. They defeat Arkansas 35–24 in the Belk Bowl. The ACC picks Fuente as its coach of the year.

2004 2006 2007 2015 2016

QUICK STATS

PROGRAM INFO*
Virginia A&M College (1892–1895)
Virginia A&M College and Polytechnic
    Institute (1896–1944)
Virginia Polytechnic Institute (1944–1969)
Virginia Polytechnic Institute and State
    University (1970–present)

KEY COACHES
Frank Beamer (1987–2015)
    238–121–2; 11–12 (bowl games)
Jerry Claiborne (1961–70)
    61–39–2; 0–2 (bowl games)
Bill Dooley (1978–86)
    63–38–1; 1–2 (bowl games)

OTHER ACHIEVEMENTS
Big East championships: 3
ACC championships: 4
Bowl record: 13–18

HOME STADIUM
Lane Stadium (1965–)

KEY PLAYERS
(POSITION; SEASONS WITH TEAM)
Hunter Carpenter (HB/K, 1900–03, '05)
Carroll Dale (WR, 1956–59)
Antonio Freeman (WR, 1991–94)
Shayne Graham (K, 1996–99)
DeAngelo Hall (DB, 2001–03)
Frank Loria (DB, 1965–67)
Bryan Randall (QB, 2001–04)
Bruce Smith (DL, 1982–84)
Tyrod Taylor (QB, 2007–10)
Michael Vick (QB, 1999–2000)

*statistics through 2017 season

For nearly 20 years, one of the big traditions of Virginia Tech football has been for the team to run out to the field at Lane Stadium as the song "Enter Sandman" plays. The song is by the hard-rock band Metallica, and the Hokies have done this since 2000. Also before each game, the players and coaches go through a tunnel to get to the field (named Worsham Field). They run under a "Hokie Stone" which they touch for good luck.

Some Virginia Tech students and Corps of Cadets members constructed a cannon in 1963. Students at the school called the cannon "Skipper" in honor of President John F. Kennedy, a former naval officer, who was assassinated in November 1963. The cannon fires outside the stadium when Hokie Village opens after the national anthem and any time Virginia Tech scores.

"True story. Our starting linebacker and our starting defensive end both tore [knee ligaments] chasing Michael Vick. It's nearly impossible to tackle him one-on-one. He's fast, he's strong, he's explosive and he loves the game of football." —Mario Edwards, a defensive back on the 1999 Florida State team that beat Virginia Tech in the Sugar Bowl to win the national championship that season.

GLOSSARY

All-American
Designation for players chosen as the best amateurs in the country in a particular sport.

conference
A group of schools that join together to create a league for their sports teams.

draft
A system that allows teams to acquire new players coming into a league.

independent
A school that is not part of an athletic conference.

legacy
Something of importance that came from someone in the past.

mascot
A character that is meant to represent a team, or a person who dresses up as that character to entertain fans.

recruiting
Convincing a student to attend a certain college, usually to play sports.

rivals
Players or teams who have a fierce and ongoing competition.

roster
A list of players who make up a team.

special teams
The players on the field for kicking and punting plays.

tainted
Polluted, or negatively affected by a negative event or quality such as a scandal.

upset
An unexpected victory by a supposedly weaker team or player.

FOR MORE INFORMATION

ONLINE RESOURCES

Booklinks
NONFICTION NETWORK
FREE ONLINE NONFICTION RESOURCES

To learn more about the Virginia Tech Hokies, visit abdobooklinks.com. These links are routinely monitored and updated to provide the most current information available.

BOOKS

Beamer, Frank, with Jeff Snook. *Let Me Be Frank*. Chicago, IL: Triumph Books, 2013.

Colston, Chris. *Tales from the Virginia Tech Sideline: A Collection of the Greatest Hokies Stories Ever Told*. New York: Sports Publishing, 2012.

Harris, Mike. *Game of My Life: Virginia Tech Hokies: Memorable Stories of Hokie Football & Basketball*. New York: Sports Publishing, 2015 (new edition).

PLACES TO VISIT

Lane Stadium
185 Beamer Way
Blacksburg, VA 24060
540-231-6731
www.hokiesports.com/football/lanestadium.html

This has been the Hokies' home stadium since 1965. The stadium is named after Edward H. Lane, the man who headed an educational foundation project that raised more than $3 million to help build the stadium. Check with the athletic department for information on tours.

INDEX

ABOUT THE AUTHOR

Jeff Seidel has been a journalist in the Baltimore-Washington area for more than 30 years. He lives there with his wife, two children, and two very faithful cats.